GIRAFFES
Towering Tall

Lucy Sackett Smith

PowerKiDS
press™
New York

For Sean Keating

Published in 2010 by The Rosen Publishing Group, Inc.
29 East 21st Street, New York, NY 10010

First Edition

Editor: Nicole Pristash
Book Design: Kate Laczynski
Photo Researcher: Jessica Gerweck

Photo Credits: Cover, pp. 1, 7, 11 Shutterstock.com; p. 5 Darrell Gulin/Getty Images; p. 9 Getty Images; pp. 12, 13 Sergio Pitamitz/Getty Images; p. 15 Ann & Steve Toon/Getty Images; p. 17 Heinrich van den Berg/Getty Images; p. 19 Art Wolfe/Getty Images; p. 21 © Peter Johnson/Corbis.

Library of Congress Cataloging-in-Publication Data

Smith, Lucy Sackett.
  Giraffes : towering tall / Lucy Sackett Smith. — 1st ed.
    p. cm. — (Mighty mammals)
  Includes index.
  ISBN 978-1-4042-8103-5 (library binding) — ISBN 978-1-4358-3267-1 (pbk.) —
ISBN 978-1-4358-3268-8 (6-pack)
  1. Giraffe—Juvenile literature. I. Title.
  QL737.U56S58 2010
  599.638—dc22
                                    2009000489

Manufactured in the United States of America

CONTENTS

So Very Tall

Do you know what Earth's tallest animal is? It is the giraffe. Giraffes are so tall that they could easily look into the second floor of a building! A giraffe's height allows it to find food that other animals cannot reach. Full-grown male giraffes are the tallest of all giraffes. These animals can grow to be 19 feet (6 m) tall!

Giraffes look like no other animal on Earth. They are known for their long, thin legs and necks. A giraffe's front legs are longer than its back legs. This gives giraffes their own special gait. A gait is an animal's way of walking and running.

Giraffes and zebras, shown here, share the same habitat, or living space. Some giraffes are four times as tall as zebras!

Getting to Water

Giraffes live on Africa's savannas. Savannas are grasslands with few trees. Giraffes live on parts of the savanna where acacia trees grow. These trees have small leaves and thorns. Acacia leaves are the food giraffes like best.

Most savanna animals must stay near water to have enough to drink. However, giraffes get most of the water they need from acacia leaves. This is good, because it is hard for giraffes to lean over to drink. Giraffes' legs are so long that they must spread them wide to lean over. This makes it easy for **predators** to creep up on drinking giraffes.

Even though giraffes are very tall, they have learned how to bend their legs so that they can reach water.

A Pattern of Shapes

Along with their height, one of the first things that people notice about giraffes is the interesting **patterns** on their coats. Giraffe coats may have a mostly reddish brown, orange, or nearly black color. White lines break this into many different shapes. Giraffes from one **area** generally have patterns and coat colors that look somewhat alike. However, every giraffe has a pattern that is a little different.

A giraffe's coat may be eye-catching to us, but **scientists** believe the pattern acts as **camouflage**. The coat colors are like those of the savanna grasses. The lines break up the tall animal's shape.

The pattern on this giraffe's coat helps the giraffe mix in with the savanna's colors.

Hard Heads, Big Hearts

On the tops of their heads, giraffes have small horns. The proper name for these horns is ossicones. Ossicones are bits of bone that stick out and are covered with fur. While female giraffes generally have just one pair of ossicones, males often have two. Giraffes, more often male giraffes, often push each other with their heads. Their hard ossicones keep the animals' heads safe.

As all **mammals** do, giraffes have hearts that pump, or push, blood through their bodies. Since giraffes are so tall, they need extra large hearts. A giraffe's heart weighs a very heavy 25 pounds (11 kg)!

Here you can see a young giraffe's ossicones. Some ossicones can grow to be 10 inches (25 cm) long!

MIGHTY FACTS

1 Giraffes have seven bones in their necks, just as people do. However, a giraffe's neck bones are much longer than a person's are.

2 There are nine subspecies, or kinds, of giraffes. These subspecies are closely related, but look a little bit different from each other.

3 Male giraffes are known as bulls. Females are called cows.

4 Giraffes have the longest tails of all mammals. A giraffe's tail can be 8 feet (2.4 m) long!

5 Scientists think giraffes sleep only about 30 minutes each day! Giraffes often take several 5-minute naps, though.

6 You can sometimes see birds called oxpeckers on a giraffe's back. These birds are very useful. They eat the bugs on a giraffe's skin!

7 Giraffes have very long **tongues**. A giraffe's tongue is generally between 18 and 20 inches (46–51 cm) long.

8 Giraffes live as long as 25 years in the wild.

In the mornings and evenings, giraffes look for food. Giraffes mix together with other giraffes. Many animals stay away from others of their kind, but giraffes happily share their land with other giraffes.

Giraffes **roam** across the savanna in groups. Some groups are made up of just males. The males in these groups **spar** with each other for **dominance**. Other groups have just females and their babies. There are also groups with a mix of males and females of all ages. The members of giraffe groups change often because the groups break up and new groups form.

During a sparring match, giraffes generally do not hurt each other. The match ends when one giraffe gives up.

Big Babies

One reason male giraffes spar for dominance is to win the right to **mate** with nearby females. Over a year after a male and female giraffe have mated, a calf, or baby giraffe, is born. Giraffe calves start walking just 15 minutes after they are born. When a giraffe is born, it is already 6 feet (2 m) tall. That is the same height as a tall man!

Young giraffes drink their mothers' milk and grow quickly. When their mothers go off to find food, calves stay with other young giraffes. These groups of young giraffes are called nursery herds.

Young giraffes must stay with their herds to keep safe. If they walk away, they may get lost or hurt.

Eating Up High

Giraffes eat plants. They most often eat acacia leaves. However, giraffes also eat the fruit, seeds, flowers, and leaves of other trees. A giraffe's height allows it to feast on plants that other animals cannot reach.

Though they sometimes eat other plants, giraffes are well suited for eating acacias. Giraffes have long, dark blue tongues. They use their tongues to reach around acacia thorns and pull leaves into their mouths. Scientists think the blue color keeps giraffes' tongues from getting sunburned while they feed. Giraffes bite off acacia branches and use their teeth to crush, or squash, the plant's thorns.

This giraffe is eating an acacia leaf. Some male giraffes eat up to 145 pounds (66 kg) of food each day!

A Giraffe's Enemies

Many predators share the giraffe's savanna home. Crocodiles sometimes **attack** giraffes from the water. The only land animals that hunt adult giraffes are lions. Other predators generally stay away from grown-up giraffes. They know that trying to kill these huge animals is not a good idea. Giraffes are fast runners, so they often just run away from predators. A giraffe can run 30 miles per hour (48 km/h).

Giraffes also fight back against predators that attack them or their babies. Giraffes use their long, strong legs to kick predators. A giraffe's kick can even break a predator's bones.

This lion has just killed a giraffe. Lions are skilled hunters, so they can easily attack an adult giraffe.

Giraffes in a Changing World

Though they can fight off many predators, there is nothing giraffes can do about the changes that are happening to their savanna home. In some parts of Africa, people are building towns and farms on land where giraffes once lived.

While disappearing savannas are a problem, the giraffe **population** is doing better than the populations of many other big African animals. Scientists believe there are around 100,000 giraffes today.

People around the world love giraffes. People even travel thousands of miles (km) to Africa to see these huge animals in person. Let's hope giraffes will always roam Africa's savannas!

GLOSSARY

area (ER-ee-uh) A certain space or place.

attack (uh-TAK) To charge at.

camouflage (KA-muh-flahj) A color or shape that looks like what is around something and helps hide it.

dominance (DO-muh-nunts) Being in charge.

mammals (MA-mulz) Warm-blooded animals that breathe air and feed milk to their young.

mate (MAYT) To come together to make babies.

patterns (PA-turnz) The colors and shapes that appear over and over again on something.

population (pop-yoo-LAY-shun) The number of animals or people living somewhere.

predators (PREH-duh-terz) Animals that kill other animals for food.

roam (ROHM) To move around from place to place.

scientists (SY-un-tists) People who study the world.

spar (SPAR) To have a practice fight.

tongues (TUNGZ) Parts inside mouths used to eat, make sounds, and swallow.

INDEX

WEB SITES

Due to the changing nature of Internet links, PowerKids Press has developed an online list of Web sites related to the subject of this book. This site is updated regularly. Please use this link to access the list: www.powerkidslinks.com/mamm/giraffe/